ALPINES

ALPINES

AN ILLUSTRATED GUIDE TO VARIETIES, CULTIVATION AND CARE, WITH
STEP-BY-STEP INSTRUCTIONS AND OVER 175 INSPIRING PHOTOGRAPHS

Christopher Grey-Wilson

Photography by Jonathan Buckley

southwater

This edition is published by Southwater
an imprint of Anness Publishing Ltd
108 Great Russell Street, London WC1B 3NA
info@anness.com

www.southwaterbooks.com; www.annesspublishing.com

If you like the images in this book and would like to investigate
using them for publishing, promotions or advertising, please visit
our website www.practicalpictures.com for more information.

© Anness Publishing Ltd 2015

A CIP catalogue record for this book is available from the British Library.

Publisher: Joanna Lorenz
Project Editor: Emma Hardy
Illustrator: Rob Highton
Designer: Ian Sandom
Production Controller: Pirong Wang

PUBLISHER'S NOTE
Although the advice and information in this book are believed to be accurate and true at the time
of going to press, neither the authors nor the publisher can accept any legal responsibility or liability
for any errors or omissions that may have been made nor for any inaccuracies nor for any loss,
harm or injury that comes about from following instructions or advice in this book.

■ HALF TITLE PAGE
Geranium dalmaticum
■ FRONTISPIECE
An alpine garden
■ TITLE PAGE
Helianthemum 'Fairy'
■ RIGHT
Edraianthus serpyllifolius 'Alba'

■ OPPOSITE TOP LEFT
Erodium variabile 'Bishop's Form'
■ OPPOSITE TOP RIGHT
Primula marginata
■ OPPOSITE BOTTOM LEFT
Origanum 'Barbara Tingey'
■ OPPOSITE BOTTOM RIGHT
Sisyrinchium 'Californian Skies'

Contents

Introduction

*A*lpines are among the gems of the plant world. Small, bright and colourful, alpines can be found in flower from the last days of winter to late autumn, providing a wealth of interest through the seasons. Since many are small, they are eminently suitable for today's restricted gardens.

Alpines are ideal for growing in troughs and containers; where space allows, a rock garden or raised bed can be built. This will provide a feature of lasting interest that will be an integral part of the overall design of the garden.

This book provides an insight into the world of alpine plants. The photographs reveal the wide range of readily available and easily grown alpines to entice the gardener, while practical advice on growing them will ensure success in your own garden.

■ RIGHT
Houseleeks (*Sempervivum*), are ideal for dry, rocky conditions.

What is an alpine plant?

Many gardeners have an image of small, brightly coloured flowers with disproportionately large blooms when they think of alpines. This is, however, only partly accurate, for alpine plants cover a wide spectrum of size and form, and it is almost impossible to come up with a 'typical' alpine.

As far as botanists are concerned, alpines are strictly those plants that grow on the mountains above the tree line in realms of harsh and exposed habitats. In the Himalayas the tree line may be at altitudes of 3660–4000m (12–13,000ft), but towards the North and South Poles the tree line (if one exists at all) can be close to sea level. Alpines can, therefore, be found at both low and

high altitudes, depending on where you are in the world. The essential feature many alpines have in common is that in the wild they grow in open and exposed places, often on rocky or stony terrain, and this, as we shall see, is important when it comes to their successful cultivation.

In practical terms, any small, hardy plant – whether it is strictly an alpine or a small plant from coastal or lowland rocky places – may be included under the general title 'alpine'. This is the definition to which most gardeners adhere, and this is the definition used in this book.

The majority of alpine plants are perennials, and they are often long-lived. Interestingly, although small

annuals and bulbs are frequently grown with alpines and are delightful additions to the alpine garden, they are rarely found in alpine regions of the world.

Alpine plants may be divided into a number of categories, as follows.

Cushion

Many alpines from high altitudes have a dense cushion habit, often described as a 'bun'. The cushion consists of numerous shoots, which are crammed together and which terminate in small, often tiny, rosettes of leaves. The flowers are borne directly on the surface of the cushion or are held well above the foliage on long stalks. Cushion alpines are typical of high alpine habitats, especially rocky slopes, moraines (glaciated areas covered by rocks and other debris) and cliffs.

Tuft

A common form of many alpines is a low, leafy tuft that bears flowers at the stem tips. The tufts are usually

■ LEFT
Veronica prostrata carpets the ground with blue or purplish flowers during the summer. It is an excellent and reliable alpine.

■ BELOW
The small shrub *Pinus mugo* 'La Cabana'
is an excellent dwarf evergreen.

herbaceous, with the stems dying down at the end of each season and new shoots arising in spring from the old base or from below ground. Tufted alpines are typical of high-altitude alpine meadows and open scrub in the mountains, some being found on more exposed rocky habitats.

Mat

The formation of a ground-hugging mat gives a plant exceptional protection in high exposed regions. The mats, which creep outwards from a centre, consist of numerous low, leafy shoots pressed close to the ground and on which the flowers are borne. Mats can grow out from a single central rootstock, or the shoots may root down as they spread. In some instances, mats are formed by a mass of underground shoots, which emerge on the surface here and there.

Rosette

Symmetrical leaf-rosettes make up some of the most appealing alpines. The rosettes can be solitary or bunched together, and they can be either long- or short-lived. The flowers, solitary or several on a

common stem, normally spring from the centre of the rosette. Rosette alpines are typical of cliffs and rocky places, but are occasionally found on high alpine meadows.

Small shrubs

In alpine regions, conditions are too bleak and exposed for all but a very

few large woody plants, and what shrubs grow there are low and mounded or spreading. Many alpine shrubs have their larger lowland counterparts – for instance, dwarf types of willows, roses, rowans, birches and junipers. These can all be found at high altitudes, especially in the European mountain ranges.

Alpines in the wild

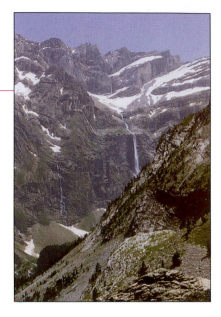

There are few greater pleasures in life than walking in the mountains, breathing in the clean, crisp mountain air and enjoying the views and the wildlife. In spring and summer the fields and slopes are full of colour and a wide variety of plants, some familiar, others less so. The variety of habitats is astonishing, and each has its own associations of plant life.

In the mountains, spring starts earliest on the lower slopes and slowly advances upwards as summer approaches. Plants in the highest habitats may not reach their spring stage until the middle of summer, and where late snow lies in the hollows spring can be considerably delayed. If you have missed spring on the lower slopes, you have only to gain altitude to reach all those delightful alpines that burst into bloom shortly after the snow melts.

Take a walk in any mountain region – in Europe, Central Asia or North America, say – and you are likely to see very similar habitats, although clearly with completely different ranges of plants. In the lower valleys there is often a stream or river bounded by lush meadows full of colourful and vigorous herbaceous plants; these are often cut for hay in the summer. On the slopes above, woods and forests of deciduous trees have an interesting array of plants on the woodland floor. Higher up the deciduous woods often give way to conifers (pines, firs and spruces), which are sometimes combined with birches and willows. Eventually the trees come to an upper limit; the tree line has been reached. Above, one enters the more exposed realm of the alpine plants. Here the slopes are steeper and rockier, and there are

■ ABOVE
Alpine plants inhabit high rocky places, such as the Cirque de Gavarnie in the French Alps.

■ LEFT
Lupins and mimulus vie for attention in the colourful mountain meadows of Mount Hood, Oregon, United States.

■ RIGHT
Geum reptans nestles against rocks in the Austrian Tyrol.

cliffs and crags, rushing streams, cascades and waterfalls.

In the right season, the high meadows are dotted with colourful, jewel-like alpines. These high meadows are often grazed by cattle or other livestock during the summer months. But the meadows are only part of the picture, for there are many other habitats, most notably the rocky ridges, screes and cliffs and, in glaciated regions, extensive moraines. All these habitats have their own particular associations of plants, many of which are specific to that habitat and are not found elsewhere. At the higher altitudes, wherever there are exposed rocks, plants can be found. At the upper extremes they are likely to be few and far between, very small and ground-hugging. Above this still are the highest peaks and ridges, which are in a world of permanent ice and snow and where no plants can survive.

Observing plants in the wild is a special pleasure. It is enchanting to see the great variety of colours and shapes of the flowers and to watch the clouds of bees and butterflies flitting from one to another. Seeing alpine plants growing in their native haunts also tells us a lot about the type of conditions they require in our gardens. Although it is excusable to pick a flower or two or take a pinch of seed to bring back for the garden, it is wholly wrong to dig up plants in the wild purely for personal gain. Plants are there for everyone to enjoy, and provided they are left alone, they will continue to thrive for future generations to experience. In addition, many countries have legislation making the removal of plants from the wild a punishable offence. Moreover, many of the most delightful mountain regions are within the boundaries of national parks and reserves, where all collecting is forbidden and where plants and animals are scrupulously protected from exploitation. None of this in any way spoils one's enjoyment of these regions – if anything, it actually enhances it.

■ LEFT
Swathes of Pyrenean broom in the high meadows on the frontier of Andorra in the Pyrenees.

Alpines in the open garden

Alpines frequently have an aura of mystique. They are often said to be difficult plants to grow and likely to appeal only to the specialist or the connoisseur of the rare and tricky. This is simply not so. Go to any good garden centre and you will see a section devoted to a colourful range of everyday alpines that are suitable for the average garden. In addition, there are numerous nurseries specializing in alpines and other small hardy plants, and the proprietors will be only too pleased to help you make a choice for the particular conditions in your own garden.

Alpines add a new dimension to the 'small and beautiful' range of plants and enrich the garden, and innumerable excellent alpine plants can be grown without the close cosseting of a frame or special alpine house.

We have seen that alpines enjoy a range of different habitats in the wild but, despite this, the majority grow in open, exposed places where, despite the often high rainfall, the ground is extremely well drained. There are, however, some alpines – some of the primulas, for instance – that enjoy more moist conditions. These

requirements can be translated into the garden environment. The majority of alpines require an open, sunny, well-drained position. Sites overhung by trees or shaded by buildings for most of the day or those that are waterlogged or badly drained are wholly unsuitable.

There is no doubt that a rock garden is one of the most attractive ways of growing alpines. The ideal site for a rock garden is one that slopes, so that excess water drains away quickly. Slopes are also easier to landscape with rocks to create the appearance of a 'natural outcrop'.

■ LEFT
A rock garden can be an exciting and attractive feature in the garden, and an integral part of the overall design.

■ OPPOSITE
A tapestry of form and colour creates an exciting feature during the summer months.

■ RIGHT
Contrasting colours make this an eye-catching rock garden.

Rock gardens (often called rockeries) can blend in well with other features in the garden and should, indeed, be viewed as an integral part of the overall design. They look particularly pleasing when juxtaposed with lawns or water features, such as a pool or stream. A well-constructed rock garden will include numerous ledges, clefts and nooks for a wide variety of alpine plants.

The rock garden, pleasing as it is, is undeniably fairly labour intensive to set up, and it can be costly to bring large amounts of rock into the garden. An alternative is to construct a scree garden, an area specially prepared with a great deal of added rock chippings or grit to improve the drainage. Alpines flourish in a well-constructed scree garden, and on flat sites, where a rock garden may seem rather inappropriate, the scree can look extremely enticing.

Some everyday alpines will flourish without any special preparation, provided the natural soil in the garden is well-drained. *Aurinia saxatilis* (syn. *Alyssum saxatile*; yellow alyssum), *Aubrieta deltoidea* (aubrieta) and *Saponaria ocymoides* (rock soapwort) will succeed perfectly well at the side of a path or driveway or the edge of the flower border.

A number of the bellflowers, including *Campanula portenschlagiana* and *C. poscharskyana*, and *Erigeron karvinskianus* (wall daisy) will colonize wall niches and cracks in paving without difficulty. These plants are very pretty in flower, but can be invasive. In dry, stony parts of the garden, *Sedum* (stonecrop) and *Sempervivum* (houseleek) will thrive for many years, revelling in neglect. Some houseleeks will succeed even on the bleak tiles of roofs where there is precious little soil, mimicking the meagre conditions in which they grow in the wild. This should not give the impression that all alpines are easy, for this is simply not the case – many demand exacting conditions in cultivation if they are to succeed – but many good alpines can be grown in the garden without too much fuss and bother.

Alpines in raised beds and walls

Raised beds and retaining walls, such as those at the edge of a lawn or patio, can make splendid places to grow alpines. The additional height above the surrounding parts of the garden gives raised areas the extra drainage that alpines need. These locations can be exciting features in the garden and important elements in the overall design and layout of the garden. It is possible to build a raised bed that will suit almost any size of garden, and they are especially convenient for gardeners who find it difficult to bend down, because they bring the plants up to a workable level and make weeding, planting and maintenance easier.

Like the rock garden, raised beds are best in the open garden in a well-lit, sunny position. However, if woodland alpines, such as trilliums and erythroniums, are to be grown, a position in the dappled shade of trees will be preferable. In practice, the beds can be any shape or size, but it is worth considering two important factors. First, if they are too wide they are difficult to manage without climbing on to them for planting and weeding, which is an important consideration for physically challenged gardeners. Second, if they are too large they will be expensive to construct and will require a great deal of compost (soil mix) to fill them.

Raised beds can be constructed from a variety of materials. Old railway sleepers are comparatively inexpensive, and they can be used to make an effective bed very quickly. A drawback, however, is that they lend themselves only to rather rigid, geometric designs. Raised beds made from brick or natural stone offer

■ ABOVE
Wall crevices provide a niche enjoyed by many rock-loving alpines such as *Campanula porskyriana*.

■ LEFT
A retaining wall or raised bed gives ideal drainage for many alpines. Here, rock roses (*Helianthemum*) are basking in the sun.

■ BELOW
Dry-stone retaining walls can act like an
extra flowerbed for alpine crevice dwellers.

more flexibility, and there is the
possibility of adding curves to the
shape of the bed. Bricks must be
frostproof and will have to be
mortared. Rocks – hard limestone
or sandstone are ideal – can be used
without mortar as dry-stone walling.
Gaps can be left in brick or stone
walls and plants incorporated in the
crevices, which can greatly add to
their appeal. Retaining walls can
be treated in a similar manner.

Raised beds can be filled with
a standard alpine compost, and
the top can then be decorated with
rock outcrops and finished off
with rock chippings.

The height of a raised bed will
depend on one's own needs and the
overall garden design, but generally
they can be anything from 20–75cm
(8–30in) tall. The higher extreme is
a comfortable working height for
wheelchair-bound gardeners. Of
course, the taller the walls of the
raised bed, the more expensive the
bed will be to build and fill with
compost and plants.

■ RIGHT
**It is important to choose the right types
of alpine plants in your raised bed. This
one contains *Edraianthus serpyllifolius*
(blue), *Aethionema grandiflorum* (pink),
and *Linum capitatum* (yellow).**

A well-constructed raised bed will
suit a wide variety of different alpines,
which will give colour and enjoyment
for many years. It will offer the
opportunity to create niches for
different types of alpines, such as
shade- or acid-loving plants, and
dwarf shrubs will give the beds extra
height and interest, especially during
the winter months.

You should avoid planting robust
alpines, such as aubrieta, shrubby
candytuft and yellow alyssum, in
raised beds, however, because they
will quickly overrun the other, choicer
plants. Prolific self-seeders should be
avoided for the same reason.

Alpines in troughs, sinks and other containers

A container brimful with colourful little alpines can be a real focal point in the garden. Placed on a patio or on the edge of a terrace or lawn, a well-planted container can add interest for many months of the year.

Containers come in all sorts of shapes and sizes, but for alpines the best by far are stone sinks and troughs. Old sinks are scarce today and therefore very expensive, but new ones are being made out of stone and also other materials, including terracotta and cement, and these are often readily available at garden centres and nurseries.

Alternatively, troughs can be constructed at home relatively cheaply using a hypertufa mix. Hypertufa, which simulates natural rock, can be very effective. It is made from one part per volume of coarse sand or fine grit, one part cement, and two parts sphagnum peat, which is mixed into a stiff paste.

Old glazed sinks can be coated with hypertufa mix to make them look like a stone trough. The same mix can be applied over the surface to a depth of about 2cm(¾in). In order for the hypertufa to stick properly to the sink, roughen the surface with a

scourer, such as a glass-cutter, and coat the surface to be covered with a bonding agent, such as epoxy resin.

Properly constructed, hypertufa will last for many years, and after a while it will become embellished with mosses and lichens, as real rock does, to make it look authentic.

Troughs are miniature gardens. Each is an individual creation that can be enhanced with small rocky outcrops, slow-growing dwarf shrubs (especially conifers and daphnes) and a variety of exciting little alpines. They can be fascinating to create, and little niches and pockets can be made

■ ABOVE

A stone trough can be very effective with a single group of plants; here houseleeks (*Sempervivum*) grow between slate shards.

■ LEFT

A group of stone troughs makes an interesting garden feature; each is a unique miniature garden of lasting interest over many months of the year.

MAKING A TROUGH

1 Use two boxes for the inner and outer moulds, allowing for walls 5–7.5cm (2–3in) thick. Coat the inside of the outer mould and the outside of the inner mould with oil to prevent the hypertufa from adhering to them.

2 The base and sides of the trough should be reinforced with fine-mesh wire netting, which can be worked into a trough shape that will fit midway between the outer and inner moulds.

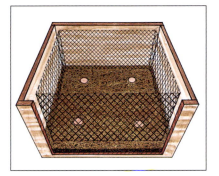

3 Place about 2.5cm (1in) of hypertufa mix in the base of the outer mould, firm down and level carefully, then place in the wire mesh. Add a further 2.5cm (1in) of hypertufa. Push through several base-depth pieces of broom handle to create drainage holes. These can be left until the hypertufa has set firmly.

4 Put the inner mould inside the outer one, and fill the space between the sides with more hypertufa mix. Firm down well and evenly to eliminate all air pockets.

5 Once it is firmly set, remove the moulds and carefully knock out the drainage plugs. Roughen the outer surface of the trough with a stiff wire brush, and round off the edges to give the trough a more natural look.

6 Compact alpines such as *Antennaria dioica* 'Minima' are ideal for planting in troughs. For added contrast and variety, try introducing a few small conifers or miniature shrubs as well.

to accommodate the different plants. Crevices between adjacent rocks are particularly valuable for alpines such as saxifrages. Troughs can be filled with standard alpine compost (soil mix) or with different compost to suit different types of alpines. For

instance, a humus-based mixture will be suitable for small ferns, ramondas and dwarf willows, while a trough filled with an acid growing medium will be ideal for ericaceous plants such as dwarf rhododendrons, cassiopes and autumn gentians.

It can also be fun to plant a trough with a single group of plants – one filled with different kinds of *Sempervivum* (houseleek) or encrusted saxifrages can be very appealing, and will provide lasting interest throughout the year.

Plant Directory

The following alpines are all comparatively easy to grow, and most of them are perennials. If you are unable to find any of these plants at a garden centre, check the pages of the current edition of the *RHS Plant Finder* for a suitable source or for the nearest specialist nursery. The height and spread indicated at the end of each entry are those each plant is likely to achieve given good cultivation. They may vary according to soil type, climate and season.

■ ABOVE
ACHILLEA AGERATIFOLIA

This charming little evergreen milfoil comes from the mountains of the Balkans. The white flowerheads, 2.5cm (1in) across, are generally solitary, but sometimes two or three are clustered together. They are borne in mid-summer on stems above the tufts of slender, finely toothed, grey-green leaves. Height 15–20cm (6–8in), spread 20–30cm (8–12in).

■ ABOVE
AETHIONEMA GRANDIFLORUM (SYN. *A. PULCHELLUM*)

Commonly known as Persian stonecrop, this is a species from western Asia, where it inhabits dry, rocky places in the wild. Plants form intricately branched tufts with numerous narrow, grey-green, evergreen leaves. The clusters of small, pink flowers are borne in late spring and early summer. If they are clipped back the moment they cease flowering, plants will generally produce a second flush of bloom in late summer. Height and spread 20–30cm (8–12in).

■ ABOVE
ALYSSUM SPINOSUM 'ROSEUM'

A densely branched little shrublet, with small, elliptical, greyish leaves, it explodes in late spring into a mass of deep pink flower clusters. In the wild it is a plant of mountain rocks and screes in southern Spain and North Africa. The species was formerly known as *Ptilotrichum spinosum*. Height and spread 30–50cm (12–20in).

■ ABOVE

ANDROSACE SEMPERVIVOIDES
(SYN. *A. MUCRONIFOLIA*)

An evergreen, mat-forming alpine from the western Himalayas. The mats consist of numerous small, neatly formed, deep green leaf-rosettes, which sport further rosettes on short, strawberry-like runners. The rounded clusters of small, mauve-pink to mid-pink flowers are held above the rosettes on short stalks. Height 5–7.5cm (2–3in), spread 15–30cm (6–12in).

■ ABOVE

ANEMONE MULTIFIDA
(SYN. *A. MAGELLANICA*)

This is a tufted perennial which has deeply divided, dark green, rather lustrous leaves. In early summer, the stiff, erect stems bear one or several white or cream, bowl-shaped flowers, each up to 2.5cm (1in) across. It is native to the Americas. Height 20–35cm (8–14in), spread 10–15cm (4–6in).

■ ABOVE

AQUILEGIA FLABELLATA
(SYN. *A. AKITENSIS*)

This delightful little alpine columbine has neat, grey-green, divided foliage. The typical flowers are purple-blue with white tips to the petals. They are borne in late spring and early summer, and will seed around in the garden. Height 40–50cm (16–20in), spread 15–20cm (6–8in). The form *A. f.* var. *pumila* f. alba (syn. 'Nana Alba') is only 15cm (6in) tall.

■ LEFT

ARABIS ALPINA
SUBSP. *CAUCASICA*
(SYN. *A. CAUCASICA*)

The common arabis of gardens comes from the Balkans and western Asia. It is a mat-forming evergreen with close, rather coarse rosettes of greyish-green leaves, and bears clusters of white flowers in spring and early summer. Double-flowered ('Flore-pleno') and variegated-leaved ('Variegata') forms are available. Height 15–25cm (6–10in), spread 20–40cm (8–16in).

■ ABOVE

ARENARIA BALEARICA

Commonly known as Corsican sandwort, this tight mat-forming plant from the Balearic islands is suitable for shaded, damp, rocky places in the garden. In spring and summer, the mats of tiny, deep green leaves bear solitary white flowers, not more than 1cm (½in) across, on wiry stems. Height 2.5–5cm (1–2in), spread 20–30cm (8–12in).

■ ABOVE

ARMERIA MARITIMA (SYN. A. VULGARIS)

The common thrift of coastal rocks and cliffs throughout much of western Europe is, in fact, native to much of the Northern Hemisphere as well as to South America. The familiar, tough, evergreen hummocks of slender, deep green leaves bear long-stalked heads of pink to reddish-purple flowers in summer. Height and spread 15–25cm (6–10in).

■ ABOVE

AUBRIETA DELTOIDEA

The familiar aubrieta of gardens, this is an evergreen, mat-forming plant with close, deep green or grey-green foliage of lax leaf-rosettes. The clusters of reddish-purple, violet, mauve or pink flowers are borne in spring and intermittently through summer. It is native to south-eastern Europe. Height 10–15cm (4–6in), spread 15–50cm (6–20in).

■ ABOVE

AURINIA SAXATILIS
(SYN. ALYSSUM SAXATILE)

The familiar yellow alyssum of gardens is an evergreen sub-shrub with large tufts of greyish- or whitish-green leaves. In spring and through summer, the plants produce sprays of tiny, yellow flowers. It is native to dry, rocky places in central and southern Europe. Height 20–30cm (8–12in), spread 30–50cm (12–20in).

■ ABOVE

CAMPANULA CARPATICA

This widely grown herbaceous bellflower from the Carpathian mountains forms small tufts with numerous, rather bright green, oval, sharply toothed leaves. The upright, broad bell-shaped flowers, 2.5–4cm (1–1½in) across, are violet, purple, blue or white, and appear in summer and autumn. Height and spread 20–30cm (8–12in).

■ ABOVE

CAMPANULA COCHLEARIIFOLIA

Often known as fairies' thimbles, this dainty little bellflower forms spreading mats by means of underground rhizomes. The small, rounded to oval leaves are bright, lustrous green, and the thin stems bear several small, nodding bells in blue, lilac, lavender or, occasionally, white. It is native to the mountains of Europe. Height 7.5–13cm (3–5in), spread 15–40cm (6–16in).

■ ABOVE

CAMPANULA PORTENSCHLAGIANA

An excellent bellflower for rock crevices or for colonizing old walls, this hails from the western part of the former Yugoslavia, as its common name, Dalmatian bellflower, suggests. The tufts of small, oval to heart-shaped leaves are bright green, and during early summer, the numerous branched stems bear a profusion of lilac-blue, rather narrow, bell-shaped flowers. Height 15–25cm (6–10in), spread 15–50cm (6–20in).

■ ABOVE

CHIASTOPHYLLUM
OPPOSITIFOLIUM
(SYN. *C. SIMPLICIFOLIUM,*
COTYLEDON SIMPLICIFOLIA)

An attractive tufted, evergreen, succulent alpine from the Caucasus mountains, this has paired, rounded to elliptical, bright green, fleshy leaves. The small, yellow flowers are borne in branched spikes, which droop at the tip. Height 15–20cm (6–8in), spread 15–30cm (6–12in).

■ ABOVE

CORYDALIS FLEXUOSA

This is a widely available Chinese species that is suitable for a semi-shaded spot and a moist, humus-rich soil. The tufts of grey-green or bright green, fern-like, dissected leaves are present though most of the year, except high summer. The sprays of blue or lilac-blue, spurred flowers are borne on wiry, branched stems in spring and early summer. Height 20–30cm (8–12in), spread 20–50cm (8–20in).

■ ABOVE

CORYDALIS LUTEA
(SYN. *PSEUDOFUMARIA*
LUTEA)

An excellent plant for crevices, this often self-sows profusely in the garden. It is a tufted, evergreen perennial with rather fleshy, grey-green, dissected leaves. The pale stems bear small sprays of yellow, spurred flowers from spring until autumn. Height 20–30cm (8–12in), spread 20–30cm (12–20in).

■ ABOVE

CREPIS RUBRA

An annual or biennial, commonly known as pink hawksbeard, the simple basal rosette is of rather dandelion-like leaves. In summer, pink or white dandelion-like flowers appear, each 2.5cm (1in) across, and borne one to a stem from the centre of the leaf-rosette. It is native to south and south-east Europe. Height 25–35cm (10–14in), spread 20–30cm (8–12in).

■ ABOVE

DIANTHUS ALPINUS

A delightful little alpine pink, this forms a small, evergreen mat of deep green, narrow, yet blunt, leaves. The relatively large, fringed flowers, 2.5cm (1–1½in) across, are pink to cerise or purplish-pink, with generous speckling above. It is native to the eastern Alps. Height 5–10cm (2–4in), spread 10–25cm (4–10in).

■ ABOVE

DIANTHUS DELTOIDES

The maiden pink, as this is commonly known, is a mat-forming, evergreen perennial with numerous narrow, deep green leaves that are often flushed with bronze or purple. The spreading, branched stems bear numerous small, fringed flowers in pink, cerise, crimson or white in summer and autumn. It is native to Europe and western Asia. Height 15–25cm (6–10in), spread 30–50cm (12–20in).

■ ABOVE

DRABA AIZOIDES

A small, tufted, evergreen alpine, commonly known as yellow whitlow grass, with deep green, crammed leaf-rosettes. The narrow, pointed leaves have sharp bristles. In spring and early summer, butter-yellow flowers are held just clear of the foliage on short stems. It is native to the mountains of central and southern Europe. Height 5–10cm (2–4in), spread 10–20cm (4–8in).

■ ABOVE

EDRAIANTHUS SERPYLLIFOLIUS
(SYN. WAHLENBERGIA SERPYLLIFOLIA)

A tufted relation of the harebells, this has a mass of narrow, deep green, spoon-shaped leaves. In summer, the centre of the plant erupts into numerous, erect, dark violet, bell-shaped flowers. It originates in rock crevices in the western Balkans. Height 2.5–5cm (1–2in), spread 15–25cm (6–10in).

■ ABOVE

ERIGERON GLAUCUS

This handsome, evergreen, leafy sub-shrub, commonly known as beach aster, has rather coarse, pale bluish-green, oval leaves. In summer, numerous pale violet to lavender flowerheads are produced, each with an egg-yolk yellow centre. Native to western North America, this needs a sheltered site on the rock garden. Height 30–50cm (12–20in), spread 45–90 (18–36in).

■ ABOVE

ERIGERON KARVINSKIANUS
(SYN. E. MUCRONATUS)

This popular wall daisy is native to Mexico. Plants form lax tufts of deep green, elliptical to three-lobed leaves, borne on wiry stems. Numerous small, white daisy flowers are produced in summer and autumn, each with a yellow centre and a lilac or purple reverse. Height 20–40cm (8–16in), spread 30–60cm (12–24in).

■ ABOVE

ERINUS ALPINUS

The pygmy foxglove is native to rocky habitats in central and southern Europe, where it forms small, evergreen tufts. The neatly toothed foliage is mainly borne in small rosettes, while the rosy-purple or white flowers are clustered at the ends of short, leafy stems. Height 10–15cm (4–6in), spread 15–20cm (6–8in).

■ ABOVE

ERIOGONUM UMBELLATUM

The sulphur flower is a mat-forming, evergreen sub-shrub from the mountains of western North America. The rosetted leaves, which are rather leathery and elliptical, are deep grey-green above but white with felt beneath. The sprigs of cream to bright yellow flowers are borne above the foliage in summer. Height 10–25cm (4–10in), spread 20–50cm (8–20in).

■ ABOVE

ERODIUM PETRAEUM

An attractive relative of the geraniums from the Iberian peninsula, this forms tufts of finely dissected, rather ferny, green or grey-green foliage. The small flowers, 2.5cm (1in) across, which are borne in summer and autumn, are white to pink or purple with the upper two petals often dark-blotched. Height 15–25cm (6–10in), spread 25–50cm (10–20in).

■ ABOVE

ERODIUM VARIABILE

A neat, hummock-forming hybrid of garden origin with a mass of small, oval, grey-green leaves. The small, solitary flowers, about 1cm (½in) across, are saucer-shaped and pink or red with attractively etched veins, and they appear in summer. Height 10–15cm (4–6in), spread 15–25cm (6–10in). The plant illustrated is 'Bishop's Form'.

■ ABOVE

GENTIANA ACAULIS
(SYN. *G. KOCHIANA, G. EXCISA*)

One of the most beautiful of alpine plants, the splendid trumpet gentian, from the mountains of central and southern Europe, forms dense mats of evergreen, leathery leaves. In spring, and sometimes also in autumn, large, bell-shaped flowers in rich kingfisher-blue appear. Height 5–10cm (2–4in), spread 20–50cm (8–20in).

■ ABOVE

GENTIANA SEPTEMFIDA

An herbaceous species from the mountains of western Asia, this gentian forms discreet tufts with spreading stems, which bear pairs of elliptical, deep green leaves. One or several deep blue, bell-shaped flowers are borne at the stem tips in late summer and autumn. Height 10–25cm (4–10in), spread 20–40cm (8–16in).

■ ABOVE

GENTIANA SINO–ORNATA

This, the finest autumn-flowering gentian, comes from western China. It is an herbaceous perennial, forming small tufts of narrow, sharply pointed, deep green, rather glossy leaves. The solitary, deep blue, green- and purple-striped, bell-shaped flowers are held on the ends of the spreading stems. It needs a humus-rich, acid soil. Height 10–15cm (4–6in), spread 15–25cm (6–10in).

■ ABOVE

GENTIANA VERNA

The spring gentian is one of the great delights of the alpine garden, forming small tufts of bright green, oval foliage. In spring, the rich blue flowers appear, sporting a small, white centre. A native to the mountains of Europe, including Britain and Ireland. Height 4–7.5cm (1½–3in), spread 10–20cm (4–8in).

■ ABOVE

GERANIUM CINEREUM 'BALLERINA'

A tufted, semi-evergreen perennial, with rounded, lobed, grey-green leaves. The paired, saucer-shaped flowers are pink with an elaborate network of purple veins, and are produced in late spring and summer. Height 15–20cm (6–8in), spread 20–50cm (8–20in).

■ LEFT

GERANIUM DALMATICUM

A clump-forming, evergreen perennial, with rounded, deeply lobed, glossy green leaves. The flowers, which are borne in masses in early and mid-summer, are a rich pink with contrasting orange-red anthers. The species comes from the western Balkans. Height 1–15cm (½–6in), spread 20–50cm (8–20in).

■ ABOVE

GYPSOPHILA REPENS
'FRATENSIS'

A rather compact, evergreen, matted perennial with pairs of narrow, grey-green leaves. The slender, spreading stems bear sprays of small, pink flowers in summer. Other varieties have white, rose or lilac flowers. Originally from the mountains of central and southern Europe. Height 10–15cm (4–6in), spread 15–30 (6–12in).

■ ABOVE

GYPSOPHILA TENUIFOLIA
(SYN. *G. GRACILESCENS*)

A low-growing, hummock-forming, evergreen alpine, with a mass of grass-like, mid-green foliage. The small, white or pale pink flowers are borne aloft on delicate wiry stems in summer. It is found in the Caucasus mountains. Height 10–15cm (4–6in), spread 15–25cm (6–10in).

■ ABOVE

HORMINUM PYRENAICUM

Commonly known as dragon's mouth, this evergreen, tufted perennial comes from the Alps and Pyrenees. The deep green leaves are mainly produced in basal rosettes. From the centre of each rosette, one-sided spikes of two-lipped, deep violet-blue flowers are borne aloft on stiff, often branched, stems. Height 30–40cm (12–16in), spread 30–50cm (12–20in).

HOUSTONIA MICHAUXII
(SYN. HEDYOTIS MICHAUXII)

A mat-forming, rather invasive, evergreen perennial, with numerous, tiny, oval, grey-green leaves. The small, rather lobelia-like flowers, which are deep violet-blue or purple, are borne singly on thread-like stems above the foliage. It is native to the central southern United States. Height 2.5–5cm (1–2in), spread 20–90cm (8–36in).

■ ABOVE

LEONTOPODIUM ALPINUM

This is the edelweiss of the European mountains. It is a small, tufted perennial with narrow, greyish, felted foliage. The small button-flowerheads are clustered and surrounded by white, woolly bracts. Height 10–15cm (4–6in), spread 15–25cm (6–10in). The plant illustrated is the cultivar 'Mignon'.

■ ABOVE

LINUM ARBOREUM

A small, evergreen sub-shrub from the eastern Mediterranean, this is commonly known as shrubby flax. It has leathery, bluish-green foliage, and butter-yellow flowers, 2.5cm (1in) across, produced during the summer months. Height 25–50cm (10–20in), spread 25–60cm (10–24in).

■ ABOVE

LYCHNIS ALPINA

This charming alpine catchfly or campion is a tufted perennial with narrow, grassy foliage. Clusters of bright rose-purple flowers are held at the tops of short, leafy stems, each petal neatly notched. It is native to northern and central Europe. Height 5–15cm (2–6in), spread 5–15cm (2–6in).

■ ABOVE
MECONOPSIS CAMBRICA

The Welsh poppy is an excellent plant for semi-shaded, moist places. It is an herbaceous perennial, forming clumps of dissected, rather bright green foliage. From spring until autumn, solitary poppy flowers in yellow or orange, each 2.5–5cm (1–2in) across, are borne on slender stems above the leaf-tufts. It comes from western Europe. Height 40–60cm (16–24in), spread 30–50cm (12–20in).

■ ABOVE
OENOTHERA MACROCARPA
(SYN. O. MISSOURIENSIS)

A large-flowered, perennial evening primrose, commonly known as Ozark sundrops, which forms large, low tufts of tough, oblong, deep grey-green leaves. The bright yellow flowers, 5–7.5cm (2–3in) across, are borne on spreading stems in summer. It is native to the southern United States. Height 20–30cm (8–12in), spread 30–60cm (12–24in).

■ ABOVE
ONOSMA ALBOROSEA

This bristly, evergreen sub-shrub from western Asia has narrow, elliptical leaves and, in late spring and early summer, arched sprays of elegant, tubular flowers, which open white, then gradually change to deep pink. Height 15–25cm (6–10in), spread 25–50cm (10–20in).

■ ABOVE
ORIGANUM 'BARBARA TINGEY'

A spreading, aromatic sub-shrub with paired, bluish-green, oval leaves that are flushed with purple beneath. The hop-like flower clusters are borne at the ends of arching shoots, the small, two-lipped pink flowers being surrounded by pale green bracts. Height 10–20cm (4–8in), spread 30–50cm (12–20in).

■ ABOVE

PAPAVER ALPINUM

This species, the alpine poppy, encompasses a number of similar plants from the European mountains (found under varying names, such as *P. burseri* and *P. rhaeticum*). They are annuals or short-lived perennials with tufts of neatly dissected, grey-green, somewhat bristly foliage. The yellow, orange-red or white poppy flowers are borne on slender stems above the foliage in late spring and summer. Height 15–25cm (6–10in), spread 20–30cm (8–12in).

■ ABOVE

PENSTEMON HIRSUTUS

An evergreen perennial with deep green, somewhat shiny, elliptical foliage and, in summer, clusters of two-lipped flowers, which are pale violet with a white throat. The best form for the alpine garden is *P. h.* var. *pygmaeus*. Height 6–10cm (2½–4in), spread 20–30cm (8–12in).

■ ABOVE

PERSICARIA AFFINIS
(SYN. *POLYGONUM AFFINE*)

A mat-forming, herbaceous perennial from the Himalayas, which has horizontal, leafy stems that root down as they grow. The leaves are elliptical, deep green but paler bluish-green beneath. The tiny pink to crimson flowers are borne in dense spikes above the foliage mat in summer and autumn. Height 10–20cm (4–8in), spread 30–80cm (12–32in).

■ ABOVE

PHLOX DIVARICATA SUBSP. *LAPHAMII*
'CHATTAHOOCHEE'

This rather lax perennial has spreading, slender stems bearing pairs of pointed elliptical, deep green leaves, which are often flushed with purple. The salver-shaped flowers, which are deep lavender with a crimson eye, are produced in summer over a long season. It comes from wooded areas in North America. Height 20–35cm (8–14in), spread 30–50cm (12–20in).

■ ABOVE

PHLOX DOUGLASII

A North American plant, this low mat- or cushion-forming, evergreen perennial has small, tooth-like leaf-pairs. The fragrant, salver-shaped flowers are solitary or several clustered together close to the foliage, and they vary in colour from pink to lavender, purple, red or white. The plant illustrated is 'Boothman's Variety', which flowers in late spring and early summer. Height 7.5–15cm (3–6in), spread 10–25cm (4–10in).

■ ABOVE

PHLOX SUBULATA

Moss phlox, which is native to the eastern United States, is a mat-forming, evergreen perennial with much-branched stems and numerous linear, pointed leaf-pairs. The salver-shaped flowers, in shades of pink, purple, red or white, appear in late spring and early summer, and are borne in clusters at the shoot-tips, close to the foliage. Height 10–15cm (4–6in). Spread 30–60cm (12–24in).

■ ABOVE

PLATYCODON GRANDIFLORUS 'APOYAMA'

This clump-forming herbaceous perennial from the Far East is related to the bellflowers (*Campanula* spp.). It has erect, pale stems and oval to elliptical, somewhat toothed leaves. The deep blue flowers, 2.5–5cm (1–2in) across, open from balloon-like buds. Height 10–23cm (4–9in), spread 10–15cm (4–6in).

■ ABOVE

POLYGALA CALCAREA 'LILLET'

A compact, mat-forming, evergreen perennial with small, deep green and rather glossy elliptical leaves. The gentian-blue flowers are borne in small clusters in late spring and summer. Milkwort, as the species is commonly known, hails from west and south-west Europe. Height and spread 2.5cm (1in) 10–20cm (4–8in).

■ ABOVE
PRATIA PEDUNCULATA
(SYN. *LOBELIA PEDUNCULATA*)

This mat-forming perennial has thread-like stems that root down as they grow. The tiny rounded to oval leaves are rather pale grey-green, while the solitary, lobelia-like, blue to purple-blue flowers, about 1cm (½in) across, are borne on very slender, erect stalks. It is native to south Australia and Tasmania. Height 2.5cm (1in), spread 20–50cm (8–10in).

■ ABOVE
PRIMULA AURICULA

The common auricula, or bear's ear, is a low, tufted perennial with rosettes of deep green, rather fleshy leaves. The sweetly scented, yellow flowers, up to 2.5cm (1in) across, are clustered at the stalk-tips in spring. It is native to the Alps. Height 7.5–15cm (3–6in), spread 10–20cm (4–8in). The one shown above is a cultivar of *Primula auricula*.

■ ABOVE
PRIMULA MARGINATA

A tufted, evergreen perennial from the Alps, with rosettes of leathery, green or grey-green leaves, which are coarsely toothed and often have mealy white farina along the margin. The pink to bluish-lavender, primrose-type flowers are clustered at the end of short stalks. Height 7.5–13cm (3–5in), spread 10–20cm (4–8in).

■ ABOVE
PRIMULA VULGARIS

The common primrose is a more or less evergreen perennial with rough, elliptical, bright green leaves borne in lax basal rosettes. The fragrant, yellow flowers are borne in profusion in late winter and spring. It is native to Europe and western Asia. Many colours are available. Height 10–20cm (4–8in), spread 20–50cm (8–10in).

■ ABOVE

PTEROCEPHALUS PERENNIS
(SYN. *P. PARNASSII*)

A mat- or low cushion-forming, evergreen perennial from Greece, which has oblong, grey, downy leaves. The pink to rosy-purple, scabious-like flowerheads, 2.5–4cm (1–1½in) across, are borne close to the foliage in the summer. Height 10–15cm (4–6in), spread 20–60cm (8–24in).

■ ABOVE

PULSATILLA VULGARIS
(SYN. *ANEMONE PULSATILLA*)

The pasque flower is an anemone-like plant with tufts of finely divided, deep green, rather feathery leaves. The solitary, half-nodding to erect, bell-shaped flowers, which are borne in spring, are white, red, violet-blue or purple, opening to 4–7.5cm (1½–3in) across, and with silky hairs on the outside. It is native to Europe. Height 10–20cm (4–8in), spread 20–50cm (8–20in).

■ ABOVE

RHODANTHEMUM HOSMARIENSE
(SYN. *CHRYSANTHEMUM HOSMARIENSE,*
LEUCANTHEMUM HOSMARIENSE)

One of the most attractive daisies for the rock garden, this Moroccan plant is a hummock-forming sub-shrub. The finely dissected, silvery-grey foliage is a perfect foil for the 4cm (1½in) wide daisy flowers. It flowers in winter and spring, weather permitting. Height 15–20cm (6–8in), spread 20–50cm (8–20in).

■ ABOVE

SAPONARIA OCYMOIDES

Rock soapwort or Tumbling Ted is a mat-forming, evergreen perennial with numerous, small, oval, deep green leaves. In late spring and summer, spreading clusters of pink or purplish flowers appear. It is native to central and south-eastern Europe. Height 10–15cm (4–6in), spread 30–60cm (12–24in).

■ ABOVE

SAXIFRAGA COCHLEARIS

A mound-forming, evergreen perennial with numerous, crammed rosettes of greyish, lime-encrusted leaf-rosettes. In summer, airy sprays of dainty, white flowers, each up to 2.5cm (1in) across, are produced on slender, reddish stems. The plant is native to the south-western Alps. Height and spread 15–25cm (6–10in).

■ ABOVE

SAXIFRAGA OPPOSITIFOLIA

A dense, mat-forming evergreen alpine, commonly known as purple saxifrage, this has deep green, scale-like leaves densely clothing the spreading stems. In late winter and early spring, solitary pale pink to rich purple flowers appear close to the foliage. It is native to many cold regions in the Northern Hemisphere. Height 1–2cm (½–¾in), spread 10–30cm (4–12in).

■ ABOVE

SAXIFRAGA PANICULATA (SYN. *S. AIZOON*)

This tufted, evergreen perennial has crammed rosettes of grey-green, lime-encrusted leaves. In summer, airy sprays of small, white or cream flowers, each up to 2.5cm (1in) across, are borne on stiff, arching stalks. It is native to Europe, Canada and Greenland. Height and spread 10–30cm (4–12in).

■ ABOVE

SAXIFRAGA HYBRIDS

There are numerous small hybrid saxifrages in a wide range of colours, which flower in late winter and spring. They are ideal for the alpine garden. They form dense little cushions of small, green, grey or silvery leaves and generally bear solitary or few-clustered flowers. There are many from which to choose; the one illustrated is *Saxifraga burseriana.*

■ ABOVE

SEDUM ACRE

Wallpepper or biting stonecrop is a familiar little plant of old
walls and rooftops. It is a bright green succulent with tiny, closely
overlapping leaves. In summer, the shoot tips burst with starry,
bright yellow flowers. It is found in Europe, North Africa and
western Asia. Height 5–7.5cm (2–3in), spread 10–30cm (4–12in).

■ ABOVE

SEDUM PULCHELLUM

A laxly tufted, succulent perennial with erect to ascending
stems adorned with linear leaves. The starry pink flowers,
1cm (½in) across, are freely produced in summer. A native
to the south-eastern United States, it is often grown as an
annual. Height 5–10cm (2–4in), spread 15–25cm (6–10in).

■ ABOVE

SEDUM SPATHULIFOLIUM

A compact mat- or hummock-forming perennial with waxy,
pale bluish-green, succulent leaf-rosettes. The small, yellow,
star-shaped flowers appear in summer, and are held on stiff stems
just clear of the foliage. It comes from western North America.
Height 2.5–7.5cm (1–3in), spread 10–30cm (4–12in).

■ ABOVE

SEMPERVIVUM ARACHNOIDEUM

The cobweb houseleek is a mat- or mound-forming evergreen
perennial with numerous greyish leaf-rosettes, tipped with red and
enveloped in a cobweb of whitish hairs. The starry, pinkish-red
flowers are clustered at the top of a short, leafy stem in summer.
It is native to central and south-west Europe. Height 5–10cm
(2–4in), spread 10–30cm (4–12in).

■ ABOVE

SEMPERVIVUM MONTANUM
(SYN. *S. HELVETICUM*)

An evergreen perennial that forms low mounds of dull green, downy, succulent leaf-rosettes. The wine-red, starry flowers are borne at the tips of erect flowering shoots. It comes from central and southern Europe. Height 10–20cm (4–8in), spread 20–40cm (8–16in).

■ ABOVE

SEMPERVIVUM TECTORUM

The common houseleek is a coarse, evergreen perennial with large, succulent leaf-rosettes. The leaves are usually green or grey-green, with reddish or purplish tips. A mass of star-shaped, dull pink to purple flowers is borne on stout, leafy stems in summer. It is native to central and southern Europe. Height 20–50cm (8–20in), spread 30–60cm (12–24in).

■ ABOVE

SILENE ACAULIS

The moss campion is a widespread plant in the mountains of Europe, Asia and North America, forming bright green, moss-like cushion mats of numerous tiny leaves. In spring, the surface becomes covered in small, pale to deep pink catchfly flowers. Height 5–15cm (2–6in), spread 10–30cm (4–12in).

■ ABOVE

SILENE UNIFLORA 'DRUETT'S VARIEGATED'

Sea campion is a familiar plant of coastal rocks and cliffs in eastern Europe. Plants form lax mounds or tufts of fleshy, grey-green stems and lance-shaped leaves. The white or pale pink campion flowers, 2–2.5cm (¾–1in) across, appear in late spring and summer, borne in lax clusters just clear of the foliage. Height 10–20cm (4–8in), spread 30–60cm (12–24in).

■ ABOVE

SISYRINCHIUM 'CALIFORNIAN SKIES'

This tufted perennial has slender, iris-like leaf-fans. In summer, slender stems bear a succession of brilliant blue, star-shaped flowers that open in sunshine. Of garden origin. Height and spread 10–15cm (4–6in).

■ ABOVE

SYMPHYANDRA WANNERI

A biennial or short-lived perennial with rosettes of oval, coarsely toothed leaves, which are deep green, sometimes flushed with purple. The pyramidal sprays of violet-blue bellflowers, each 2.5–4cm (1–1½in) long, appear during the summer. It is found in south-eastern Europe. Height 20–30cm (8–12in), spread 10–20cm (4–8in).

■ ABOVE

THYMUS SERPYLLUM

An aromatic, mat-forming, evergreen perennial with masses of tiny, oval leaves. Small clusters of pink to purple flowers adorn the mats during the summer. It is native to Europe and western Asia. Height 2.5–7.5cm (1–3in), spread 10–50cm (4–20in). The plant illustrated is the cultivar 'Annie Hall'.

■ ABOVE

TROLLIUS ACAULIS

This tufted, herbaceous perennial from the western Himalayas has rather bright green, rounded, deeply lobed leaves and erect stems, bearing solitary, yellow, buttercup-like flowers, 2.5–5cm (1–2in) across. Height 10–25cm (4–10in), spread 10–20cm (4–8in).

■ RIGHT

VERONICA PROSTRATA

This mat-forming perennial has deep
green, narrow-oblong leaves. In summer,
spikes of rich blue or purplish flowers are
borne above the foliage on stiff, somewhat
leafy stems. The species comes from the
mountains of Europe. Height 10–25cm
(4–10in), spread 20–50cm (8–20in). The
plant illustrated is the cultivar 'Trehane'.

■ ABOVE

VIOLA CORNUTA

The Pyrenean pansy, or horned violet, has bright green, oval
foliage and small, 2.5–3cm (1–1¼in), pansy flowers in violet,
violet-blue or white. It self-seeds readily in the garden. It is
found in the Pyrenees and in the Pennines. Height 10–20cm
(4–8in), spread 20–30cm (8–12in).

■ ABOVE

VIOLA LUTEA

Commonly known as the mountain pansy, this tufted perennial has
bright green, oval leaves and pansy flowers, which are yellow, violet
or bicoloured, each up to 4cm (1½in) across and appearing in spring
and summer. It is native to the mountains of central and western
Europe. Height 7.5–15cm (3–6in), spread 10–20cm (4–8in).

Choosing and buying alpines

Among the greatest joys of gardening are obtaining and growing plants. Alpines are no exception, and there is a wide range from which to choose. Most good garden centres will have an area set aside for alpine plants, and if you go there during the spring and summer months, you are likely to see them in flower. This makes the choice somewhat easier, as you can see the colours and type of flower of each, which will help you make a decision. Alpine plants generally cost relatively little, but the correct choice will give you years of pleasure.

It is one thing seeing a pretty little plant in a pot in the garden centre, but it is another matter altogether whether that plant will be suitable for the conditions in your particular garden. If you are not certain, take a moment to glance at the information on the plant label. Apart from the name of the plant and a picture of it

■ BELOW
It is easy to choose plants when they are as vigorous and well-flowered as this *Helianthemum* 'Sudbury Red'.

■ BELOW
An ideal alpine purchase: strong, with
an absence of pests, diseases and weeds.

in flower, there will be a brief description of the growing conditions and the ultimate size of the plant. Some alpines require acid soils or shade, but most require neutral to alkaline soils and lots of sunshine. Although many alpines are small and discrete, some can be quite invasive and will require more room in the garden. It is no good putting the more rampant ones in troughs and containers with choice plants.

By far the best way to obtain alpines is to take the trouble to visit your nearest alpine nursery, where there will be a far greater range of exciting finds. You can locate suitable nurseries by doing online searches on the internet. Don't be inhibited by the serried ranks of alpines, each with its little plastic label, that you will find. There will be a lot of plants there suitable for your own garden. Have a word with the proprietor – alpine gardeners are friendly and generous people, and are only too keen to help and advise.

Alpines can also be obtained by mail order, but if possible go to the source and make your own selection.

It perhaps goes without saying that you should buy only healthy and vigorous young plants. Any that show signs of pests or disease or unnatural yellowing or colouring of the leaves should be rejected. Tired old plants that are past flowering or are pot-bound are also best rejected, as are the piles of left-over plants marked 'reduced to clear' that many garden centres seem to have. If plants are in flower, select those that are in bud or just opening, so that you will be able to enjoy the blooms for longer.

When you get your plants home, make sure they are adequately watered and place them in a cool place until you are ready to plant them out in their final positions.

Constructing a small rock garden

Ideas about constructing a rock garden range from aiming to achieve a 'natural' look to preferring the wholly artificial. Few gardens are lucky enough to possess a natural rocky outcrop, but such a feature can be created quite simply by carefully placing rocks to give the impression that they are rising from deep within the soil. In more formal gardens the natural look can seem totally out of place, and a more regular shape of rock garden, such as an island rock garden would be better. Alternatively, a raised bed may well be more appropriate. Whatever style is chosen,

be careful to make sure that the rock garden blends in well or complements other permanent features in the garden.

Before starting construction, make sure that the site is free of weeds, especially pernicious perennials such as couch grass and bindweed. It may, in fact, be necessary to clear the site completely over a period of weeks using weedkillers. Once the chosen site has been dug over, add sufficient grit to ensure there will be good drainage, adding proportionately more for heavier soils and less for light, sandy ones.

■ ABOVE
Rocks should be sympathetically sited to give adequate pockets for a range of different alpine plants.

POSITIONING SMALL ROCKS

1 Choose the rocks carefully, selecting the best for the most prominent part of the proposed rock garden Dig out a suitably sized pocket in the soil to provide stability for the chosen rock, aiming to bury about one-third.

2 Manoeuvre the rock into position, tilting it backwards so that the stratum lines run back into the soil, if possible. Place the other rocks in position, abutting some to give the impression of a larger rock mass, and to provide crevices for choice alpines.

3 Make sure that the stratum lines of the rock flow in the same direction, or the finished construction will look insecure and unnatural. Add rock detritus and chippings to enhance the surface of the rock garden. This can be added before or after planting. When you are planting alpines on the rock garden, follow the guidelines for troughs and sinks.

4 The completed rock garden should look like a rock outcrop or a series of outcrops with numerous crevices, pockets and ledges to accommodate the alpines.

■ LEFT
Rock gardens can be constructed on many different scales. To maneouvre rocks as large as these, you may well need to use a mechanical aid.

Types of rock

■ BELOW
**Tufa (top centre), ironstone (right)
and two types of limestone.**

Limestone

This sedimentary rock is high in calcium and is, therefore, no good for acid-loving alpines. Limestones can be hard or soft and usually have well-defined stratum lines. Soft limestones are useless for rock garden construction. For conservation purposes, avoid weatherworn surface limestone, which will have been stripped from the landscape.

Sandstone

Another sedimentary rock, sandstone can be very variable in texture and colour, although sandy colours, browns and reds are usual. The most suitable sandstone rocks are those that have well-defined stratum lines. Not only will they look more attractive in the rock garden, but they will also be easier to split if necessary.

Tufa

An ideal rock for many alpines, tufa is very porous and can be easily drilled to create holes to accommodate plants. It is also light in weight and therefore easy to transport. Mineral-rich and often high in calcium, tufa is formed where mineral-rich waters are checked – in gorges or by waterfalls. It is, however, expensive and rarely available in quantity.

Choosing rock and stone

Apart from the plants, the most important element in the rock garden is the rock itself. If the rock garden is badly built or if the wrong rock is chosen for its construction, it will never look satisfactory, and will be a constant source of disappointment every time you walk around the garden.

Rock is heavy and expensive to transport, so whenever possible acquire it locally. You should be able to find a local quarry by doing a search on the internet.

Making the right choice

It is important to bear in mind, however, that some types of rock are wholly unsuitable for rock garden construction. Featureless rocks, such as granite and ironstone, and those that weather badly, such as friable oolitic limestones and shales, should be avoided. Instead, select a hard rock with good lines (strata) and other features. Rocks with character, such as hard limestones and sandstones, are ideal, and they have the added advantage of being easy to split if that becomes necessary.

If you want a large amount of rock, it is best to buy it from a local quarry or stone merchant, where you will be able to select those rocks you want for yourself, and where it will certainly be cheaper. If you want just a few pieces, most garden centres supply various types of rocks, which are priced per piece. Remember that larger rocks are more effective in the rock garden than lots of small pieces, but this depends somewhat on how easy it is to move the rocks on to the site.

When the rock is delivered to your home, try to make sure that it is dropped as close to the rock garden site as possible; this will save a great deal of time and energy. Take care that pieces do not fall on your feet or hands, and be especially careful if children or pets are in the vicinity.

When you handle rocks, wear gloves and stout, protective boots, especially when you are moving large blocks of rock.

Moving rock and stone

When you have to move heavy rocks, always take every safeguard, and be particularly careful about not damaging your back when lifting. Large rocks can be moved small distances by levering them with iron bars or crowbars. On flat or gently

sloping ground, rocks can be placed on a wooden block and moved to the site by employing a system of rollers, which can be made from short lengths of scaffold pole or broom handle. As the rock moves over the ground, the rear rollers can be moved to the front. Large, heavy rocks can be manoeuvred into position using a block and tackle. Smaller rocks can be moved in a wheelbarrow. Those with a pneumatic tyre (tire) are ideal, and will cause least damage to lawns and pathways.

Move the largest rocks into their final position first, adding the smaller ones after you are satisfied that the 'bones' of the rock garden are satisfactory. There will always be plenty of small pieces and fragments of rock left over, and these are ideal for decorating the surface of the rock garden or for using in troughs and other containers.

MOVING LARGE ROCKS

1 Use a stout iron bar or crowbar to lever rocks short distances. A piece of wood or small rock placed under the bar will act as a fulcrum against which to lever.

2 When moving rocks a distance across the garden, use a porter's or sack truck with pneumatic tyres (tires), which will cause little damage to lawns or pathways. Use a wheelbarrow for small rocks.

3 For large, heavy rocks, a series of wooden planks or firm mats and rollers can be used. The rock is worked on to a mini-palette or tray and can be easily pushed over the rollers. As the rock progresses, the rear rollers can be moved to the front.

Alpine composts

Mixing compost (soil mix) is a bit like cooking: the ingredients have to be correct and added in the right proportions, and the mixture has to be thoroughly mixed. It is possible to mix a basic compost that will suit most alpines, whether they are grown on the rock garden, in troughs or containers, or in pots under glass.

Mixing a standard alpine compost

Remember that if the alpines that you are growing are acid-loving, such as autumn gentians and dwarf rhododendrons, then the ingredients must be calcium-free.

The basic mix can be altered to suit various groups of alpines. For instance, moisture-loving alpines, such as many primulas, can have less drainage material, while many cushion-forming alpines require even better drainage, so add more grit.

Ingredients

• Sterilized loam or a good weed-free garden soil.
• Sharp sand or fine potting grit.
• Peat or peat substitute – a friable, sieved (strained) garden compost will do well.
• Bonemeal – always use rubber gloves when handling this.

Proportions

One part (by volume) loam, two parts grit or sharp sand, one part peat and bonemeal at the rate per volume as recommended on the manufacturer's package.

Mixing

Blend the ingredients together thoroughly using a shovel. If you are mixing large quantities, a cement mixer is highly efficient. Before mixing an alpine compost, always check the individual needs of each plant to ensure the mix is suitable.

MIXING A STANDARD ALPINE COMPOST

1 Measure out the ingredients (clockwise from top right): one part peat and bonemeal, two parts grit or sharp sand and one part loam.

2 Mix the ingredients together thoroughly using a shovel. For larger quantities, a cement mixer can be very efficient.

3 Whilst this is a standard alpine compost, it is possible to alter the mix to suit different alpines. Many alpines require better drainage, so add more grit for these.

The scree garden

■ ABOVE

A scree garden with a range of plants, including *Achillea ageratifolia* **and** *Geranium cinereum* **in the foreground.**

Where a rock garden or raised bed would be out of place in the overall plan of the garden, a scree is well worth considering. Screes are generally cheaper to construct and do not require large amounts of heavy rock or brick, although they do require copious amounts of small rock fragments. A well-constructed scree planted with a host of exciting and colourful little alpines can be a captivating sight, and the envy of the neighbours.

A good scree, which is basically an area full of rock detritus which is extremely well-drained, mimics perfectly the type of conditions that many alpine plants enjoy in their wild habitats.

Scree gardens should be sited in an open, sunny part of the garden. A high point or slope is perfect, but avoid any hollows, where the drainage may be impaired and where water will collect. The selected area should be prepared by digging it out

to a depth of 20–40cm (8–16in), the greater depth being necessary on heavier, less well-drained soils. If the soil that is removed is of good quality and free of weeds, it can be used as the basis of the scree mix; if it is not, good loam or topsoil will have to be imported. About a half of the volume removed from the site should be mixed with an equal quantity of stone chippings and added bonemeal. It can then be transferred to the 'scree pit', where it should be trodden in firmly as filling proceeds. For the best results, make sure that the top 10–15cm (4–6in) of the scree bed is pure chippings and contains no soil. The surface of the scree should lie more or less flush with the

■ LEFT

Although cheaper to construct, a scree garden can be just as effective as a rock garden, and in many ways it fits in better with a modern garden environment.

■ ABOVE
Onosma alborosea makes an excellent,
long-lived scree plant.

■ RIGHT
Vivid blue gentians *(Gentiana acaulis)* vie
with willowy yellow *Aurinia saxatilis* and
sweet-scented dwarf *Narcissus* 'Baby Moon'.

surrounding garden, although
initially it can be mounded up
to allow for subsequent settling.

The type of aggregate (stone
chippings) used will depend primarily
on what can be acquired locally.
Sharp grit, pea gravel and hard
road-type grits are all suitable. Very
sharp sand is also suitable, but most
sands, especially builder's sand, will
tend to clog up the soil rather than
improve drainage, and there is always
the possibility that it could contain
harmful salt.

The surface of the scree can be
adorned with pieces of rock or
strategically positioned stepping
stones to make access easy.

Note that screes are suitable for a
wide range of alpines, but it is best
to avoid those that are too vigorous.

GOOD SCREE PLANTS

Acantholimon glumaceum	*Dianthus alpinus* (alpine pink)
Aethionema grandiflorum	*Edraianthus serpyllifolius*
(syn. *A. pulchellum;*	*Linum arboreum* (shrubby flax)
Persian stonecress)	*Onosma alborosea*
Androsace sarmentosa	*Papaver alpinum*
Armeria juniperifolia	(alpine poppy)
(syn. *A. caespitosa*)	*Silene acaulis* (moss campion)

■ ABOVE A cross-section of a scree bed. The top-dressing can be made from
stone chippings, grit or gravel.

Planting a trough or sink

Troughs and sinks should be treated like miniature gardens. They make ideal homes for many small slow-growing alpines, and each one should be regarded as an individual specimen with its own particular characteristics. Above all, however, troughs and sinks are fun to make, and hours of pleasure can be had in their creation and in the selection of suitable plants. The surface can be enhanced with pieces of rock, placed to provide various niches for the plants, and making it resemble a miniature rock garden.

When you select a trough or other container for alpines, make sure that they have adequate drainage holes at the base. If not, additional holes will need to be drilled.

Always place the container in its final position before filling it – it will become heavy and far more difficult to move once it is full of compost (soil mix). At the same time, raise the container off the ground and stand it on bricks or blocks, which not only enhances the appearance but will allow excess water to drain away quickly. Raising the container in this way also prevents worms from getting into the trough or container from the ground below.

MAKING AN ALPINE TROUGH

1 Place the trough in its final position before it is filled; otherwise, it will be too heavy to move. Troughs look best when raised off the ground by 20–30cm (10–12in), standing on bricks or concrete blocks. Make sure that they are stable and will not tip over.

2 Ensure that the trough is level and has adequate drainage holes. Place coarse drainage material over the drainage holes and the base of the trough to a depth of about 10cm (4in). Pieces of broken pot, brick or other rubble will suffice.

3 Fill the trough with a suitable alpine compost (soil mix), adding it in layers and making sure that it is firmed in adequately, especially in the corners and around the edges. Fill to 2.5cm (1in) from the top.

4 Decorate the surface with suitable pieces of rock. Angle the pieces into the compost, making sure that about one-third of each piece is buried. This will create mini-outcrops that will provide various pockets for planting the alpines.

5 Place the selected alpines in the trough, scooping out holes to take the root ball of each in turn. Firm the plants in, but avoid the temptation to over-firm. Place the larger and central plants first, finishing with those around the edges.

6 Finish off with a top-dressing of coarse grit or rock chippings, making sure they are pushed well under each alpine. Water the trough thoroughly.

7 If plants are carefully selected, a trough or sink can resemble a miniature rock garden. Add small conifers and dwarf trees to frame other plants, and miniature shrubs to provide contrasting form and colour throughout the year.

PLANTS SUITABLE FOR SUNNY, ALKALINE TROUGHS

Aquilegia flabellata

Chiastophyllum oppositifolium

Dianthus alpinus (alpine pink)

Draba aizoides (yellow whitlow grass)

Gentiana verna (spring gentian)

Juniperus communis 'Compressa'

Linum arboreum (shrubby flax)

Polygala calcarea 'Lillet'

Saxifraga cochlearis 'Minor' (and many other saxifrages)

Sempervivum arachnoideum (and many other sempervivums)

Alpines in pots

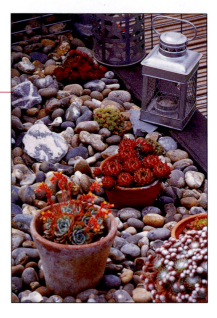

Many alpines are ideally suited to pot cultivation, and there can be no doubt that some are more successfully grown in containers under glass where the growing conditions can be more easily controlled.

This is especially true of the numerous cushion-forming alpines and small bulbs that dislike excessive moisture. Too much water during the winter months can cause cushion-forming plants to rot, while most bulbs require dry conditions in summer if they are to succeed.

Growing alpines in pots is a wonderful way to cultivate them, and if you have a greenhouse or conservatory, you can enjoy them in their containers when it is not possible to venture into the garden. It also enables you to plan late winter and spring displays of alpines and dwarf bulbs under cover.

There are several important factors to consider when growing alpines in pots under glass. First, the glasshouse or conservatory must be well-ventilated at all times, except in the worst of winter weather.

Second, even though alpines enjoy plenty of light, many will scorch under glass, especially when they are putting on new growth. To overcome this, some shading will be required.

Third, a careful watering regime must be followed, as you would for any plants under glass. It is important to understand the different requirements of the individual plants that you are growing and to learn when some, such as bulbs, need a dry break, as well as knowing which plants are best watered from the side rather than from overhead.

There are, however, many alpines that can be grown quite satisfactorily in pots under glass without too much difficulty or fuss.

■ ABOVE
Sempervivums are very easy to grow in small pots. They like a sunny, outdoor position and do not need any special care during the winter months.

■ LEFT
Numerous alpines excel when grown in pots. The vivid colours of *Primula auricula* stand out beautifully in this simple, geometrically shaped white pot.

PLANTS SUITABLE FOR POT CULTIVATION

Alyssum spinosum

Edraianthus serpyllifolius

Eriogonum umbellatum (sulphur flower)

Gentiana acaulis (trumpet gentian)

Leontopodium alpinum (edelweiss)

Lewisia cotyledon

Linum arboreum (shrubby flax)

Primula auricula (and many other primulas)

Saxifraga paniculata (and many other saxifrages)

Sempervivum tectorum (and many other sempervivums)

POTTING AN ALPINE

1 Choose a suitable pot (clay or plastic), and make sure it is clean, washing it if necessary. Avoid the temptation of selecting a pot that is too large; one that is twice the diameter of the selected plant is about right.

2 Place pieces of perforated zinc or broken pots over the drainage hole. Place a little compost (soil mix) in the lower third of the pot and firm in gently.

3 Add the plant to the pot, trying not to disturb the root ball too much. If the root ball is very congested, try teasing out some of the larger roots, but take care that you do not break them.

4 Fill in around the plant with additional compost until the level is just below the rim. Firm in gently, but avoid over-firming. Top-dress with coarse grit or rock chippings, pushing it well under the neck of the plant. Use larger pieces of rock, if necessary, especially for cushion alpines.

5 Water in the plant, preferably by dribbling water around the edge rather than watering it from overhead, which could lead to mould problems with soft-leaved and some cushion alpines.

Bulbs for the rock garden

Dwarf bulbs can be an added bonus to alpine gardening. Carefully chosen bulbs will prove excellent companion plants to alpines, and some of the smaller bulbs are, in fact, from high mountain regions of the world. Many of the dwarf bulbs – especially the crocuses, small tulips and daffodils – are bright and cheerful plants, which cannot fail to add interest. Although many bulbs flower in spring, others are summer or autumn flowering, and therefore provide colour for many months of the year.

A wide range of bulbs is available at garden centres and other outlets, and the choice can be rather bewildering. However, the packets will give details of each plant's height and flowering time, as well as when and where to plant.

As far as alpine gardening is concerned, only the smallest types are suitable, and you should limit your choice to those that do not grow more than 20cm (8in) tall. There are, however, many other factors to take into consideration. For a start, the bulbs should be fully hardy. Types that are prolific seeders or spreaders, such as many *Allium* (onion) and *Crocus tommasinianus*, are unsuitable because they will very quickly fill every pocket in the rock garden. Bulbs that have large leaves – and many develop their leaves fully only after flowering has taken place – can be very awkward among alpines because the leaves flop on top of the alpines and spoil them and, in any case, the large leaves of the bulbs can look unsightly.

PLANTING BULBS

1 Bulbs look best in close, irregular groups in the alpine garden. Scoop out a suitable hole and, if necessary, add some bonemeal. The hole should be about three times the depth of the bulb.

2 Put the bulbs in the hole, placing them at the distance apart recommended on the package. This will give them room to expand and multiply in the next few years. Make sure the bulbs are placed the correct way up – that is, with the root plate at the bottom.

3 Pull the soil back over the bulbs and firm it down, taking care not to dislodge the bulbs as you work. Leave the surface level and top-dress with rock chippings similar to the rest of the rock garden or raised bed.

■ RIGHT

Dwarf bulbs such as this snowdrop *Galanthus nivalis* are ideal 'mixers' in the rock garden or scree bed.

There are, however, numerous excellent bulbs to select, including some of the small scillas in shades of blue, many of the little crocuses, which are available in a rainbow of shades, the delightful little hardy cyclamen, which have pink, magenta or white flowers, and a host of small fritillarias with their dainty bells in reds, browns, yellows and white.

If you want to be absolutely certain about which bulbs to choose, visit a specialist alpine nursery where there will be a suitable selection of good 'alpine bulbs', including several that you are unlikely to find in an ordinary garden centre.

Dwarf bulbs can be used to very good effect in a rock garden or a raised bed, or in containers and troughs, together with a selection of attractive alpine plants. Even if you have no garden at all, you can still gain a great deal of pleasure from a window box planted with a few alpines and dwarf bulbs.

■ ABOVE

Early spring is an ideal time for the small crocuses. Here, *Crocus* 'Snow Bunting' opens its chalices to the warm spring sunshine.

BULBS SUITABLE FOR ROCK GARDENS

Allium flavum

Anemone blanda

Corydalis solida (fumewort)

Crocus chrysanthus (numerous cultivars available)

Cyclamen coum

Fritillaria meleagris (snake's head fritillary)

Galanthus nivalis (snowdrop; numerous cultivars available)

Ipheion uniflorum 'Wisley Blue'

Narcissus bulbocodium (hoop-petticoat daffodil)

Oxalis adenophylla (plant bulbs just below the surface)

Scilla mischtschenkoana

Tulipa linifolia

Propagating alpines

Propagating your own plants from seeds or cuttings is one of the most pleasurable aspects of gardening. It can be both exciting and rewarding to raise your own plants and to watch them gradually develop into their flowering maturity.

Hygiene is very important when it comes to propagating. Always use clean pots and fresh, sterilized compost (soil mix), otherwise pests and diseases may well ruin hours of patient work. Seed should be as fresh as possible, and cuttings or divisions should be pest-and disease-free as far as you can ascertain. Labelling batches of seeds or cuttings as you proceed will prevent muddle and confusion later on.

With cuttings and divisions of established plants, you can be certain that what you propagate will come true to type, but this is not always certain with seed. Many seeds will come true to type, but others will not, and some seed batches may even show a great deal of variation in the offspring. Plants such as pansies and violets (*Viola*) and the alpine columbines (*Aquilegia*) are notoriously promiscuous in the garden, and where several species or kinds of each are grown in the same garden, hybrids are certain to occur.

This can be annoying or rewarding, depending on what you want – some gardeners delight in getting variations, and there is always the possibility that something really novel and beautiful may turn up.

Taking cuttings

There are several types of cuttings:
• Softwood: the soft shoots of active young plants are generally taken in spring or early summer – aubretia, *Gypsophila repens* and alpine phlox, for example.
• Semi-ripe: firm yet not woody shoots of the current season are taken during the summer – clematis, daphne and helianthemum (rock rose), for example.
• Hardwood: firm, well-ripened, woody young shoots of the current season are taken in late summer and autumn – dwarf conifers, such as *Juniperus communis* 'Compressa' and *Salix alpina*, for example.
• Rosette: many alpines have small leaf-rosettes – androsace, many saxifrages and sempervivum, for instance – and these can be removed individually, generally with a very short length of stem. This is best undertaken in spring and summer.
• Leaf: a few alpines, such as haberlea,

ramonda and large-leaved sedums, have large leaf-rosettes, and individual leaves can be removed and treated as cuttings.
• Irishman's: pieces of plants, often individual shoots, are pulled from the base of the parent plant and already have roots attached. *Gentiana acaulis* (trumpet gentian), *Veronica peduncularis* and *Viola cornuta* can be propagated in this way.
• Root: sections of thick, fleshy roots, cut into 2.5–5cm (1–2in) sections and inserted in pots of cutting compost or sharp sand, will form new plants. This method applies to only a few alpines, including *Primula denticulata* (drumstick primrose) and *Pulsatilla* (pasque flower).

■ ABOVE
Many alpines can be readily increased by propagation methods. Here, a pot-grown *Campanula* is ready for division.

SOWING SEEDS

1 Select clean plastic pots and place a 2cm(¾in) layer of coarse grit in the bottom to cover the drainage holes.

2 Fill the pots to 1cm (½in) of the rim with a suitable seed compost (soil mix). Firm down the compost to level it, but do not over-firm.

3 Water the pots with a fine rose on the watering can. Alternatively, immerse the pots to half their depth in a basin of water. Once the compost is wet, allow the pots to drain for an hour before sowing.

4 Sow the seeds evenly and thinly over the surface. Thin sowing is essential, especially for alpine plants.

5 Sprinkle a fine layer of extra seed compost over larger seeds, followed by a thin layer of potting grit. Fine seed should be simply covered with grit.

6 Carefully label each plot with the name of the plant and the date of sowing. Place the pots in a cool, moist position outside to germinate. Once the seedlings are large enough to handle, prick out into individual pots and grow on in a cold frame or cold glasshouse.

DIVISION

1 Carefully dig up the parent plant, and gently shake off the excess soil.

2 Divide it into suitably sized sections, each with its own share of shoots and roots. Pull the pieces apart by hand or use two hand forks, held back to back, to tease the clumps apart.

3 Replant in a suitably prepared site or pot on pieces to become established. At the same time, discard any old, tired bits of plant, or those with any sign of pests or disease.

TAKING SOFTWOOD CUTTINGS

1 You will need hormone rooting powder, plastic bags, a pot filled with cuttings compost (soil mix) and secateurs (pruners).

2 Remove healthy, leafy, non-flowered shoots that are 1–6cm (½–2½in) long from the parent plant, cutting immediately below a node (leaf joint).

3 Trim off the leaves from the lower half of the stem, and dip the cut end into a hormone rooting powder.

4 Place several cuttings around the edge of a pot in cuttings compost, inserting them to about half their length.

5 Water with a suitable fungicide and leave to drain.

6 Place the pots of cuttings in a propagator or in individual plastic bags, in a light but not sunny position.

Pests and other problems

Like other plants, alpines suffer from their fair share of pests and diseases. Diligent hygiene and the routine inspection of plants for signs of attack will stave off most problems.

Aphids

How to identify: Clusters of tiny, greenish (sometimes brownish or black) insects, which may or may not have wings, concentrate at the shoot-tips or on the undersurfaces of young leaves or buds (see below). Root aphids, which live below ground, can be a serious pest of some alpines, especially primulas under glass.
Cause: Populations of winged aphids readily migrate to other plants, especially in spring and summer.
Prevention: Good hygiene and regular inspection of plants for signs of infestation. Early control will prevent the pest moving on to others.
Control: Spray with an appropriate insecticide.

Aphids

Birds

How to identify: Birds can damage plants by pecking at growing tips and buds. Tits and finches are perhaps the worst offenders, but blackbirds can disturb plants by pulling up labels in their pursuit of food.
Cause: Resident and migratory populations can cause problems, especially in winter and spring.
Prevention: Netting, bird scarers and black cotton threaded above the plants will help control the problem.
Control: Birds are a great asset to the garden by helping to control pests such as aphids and caterpillars. They should never be captured or killed.

Mice and voles

How to identify: Small rodents with long tails (mice) or short tails (voles) are familiar in many gardens. They will nibble and eat at the young shoots and buds of certain plants, and are very partial to eating bulbs.
Cause: Mice and voles burrow into banks and under sheds or in the roots of trees and shrubs, and are virtually impossible to eliminate from the garden environment.
Prevention: Good hygiene will help keep the problem under control to some extent, but in most cases a regular system of control may have to be adopted. Cats can be extremely efficient in this respect.
Control: Traps and poison baits are widely used. Many people prefer to capture rodents in humane traps and release them away from the garden. Inspect traps every day.

Red spider mite

How to identify: The minute, spider-like creatures are most readily seen under a hand lens. They are troublesome in warm, dry situations. Leaves and shoots become speckled with brown where the mites have attacked and, in bad infestations, the plant may be covered in a fine web.
Cause: Mites overwinter as adults in mild regions or as eggs. Good hygiene is essential, and any dead leaves where they may overwinter should be removed and destroyed.
Prevention: Mites dislike high humidity, so regular watering will give some control. However, many alpines dislike too much moisture, and the pest will need to be controlled once it is diagnosed.
Control: Spray regularly with a suitable insecticide (miticide) or use a biological control.

Slugs and snails

How to identify: Slugs and snails can cause a great deal of damage to seedlings and young plants.
Cause: Slugs live in the soil, under stones; snails live in rocks and in the cracks in walls. They feed primarily during the night.
Prevention: Good hygiene will give a measure of control, but encouraging animals into the garden, particularly birds, toads and hedgehogs, will be of greater benefit.
Control: Baits and various chemical controls are available, but many harm other wildlife. Beer traps and other non-chemical devices are available.

Vine weevil

How to identify: The vine weevil is one of the most serious pests of alpines. The adult weevil is a small, dark brown beetle, about 1cm (⅖in) long, with longitudinal stripes and yellow speckling. They emerge from little white-shaped grubs that live in the soil among the roots of the plants.
Cause: Vine weevils overwinter as adults in debris or as grubs in the soil, and multiply rapidly in spring.
Prevention: Practise good hygiene

and inspect regularly for adult weevils. Dispose of any infected compost.
Control: Chemical sprays are available, but biological control and vigilance are the best measures.

Botrytis (grey mould)

How to identify: This familiar fungus causes furry grey mould on leaves and stems (see below right). It may rapidly infect other parts of the plant.
Cause: The fungal spores are wind-blown and can attack plants at almost any time of the year, but particularly during damp, dull weather.
Prevention: Good hygiene is essential, and all dead or dying bits of plant should be removed.
Control: Spray at the first sign of attack with suitable fungicides (either surface or systemic).

Damping off

How to identify: A disease that attacks young seedlings, causing them to suddenly die.
Cause: Various soil-borne fungi.
Prevention: Good pot and compost hygiene, as well as thin sowing, good aeration and the avoidance of over-watering.

Control: Regular sprays with a suitable fungicide will help once the problem is noted.

Viruses

How to identify: Many different viruses attack plants, and the symptoms are varied, although blotching of the foliage, growth distortion and general weakening of the plant are often seen.
Cause: Transferred to plants through biting insects, such as aphids, or by transference by hand from one plant to another and by using infected implements, such as knives and secateurs (pruners) when propagating.
Prevention: Good hygiene is essential. Destroy all infected plants.
Control: Keep all sucking insects under control and remove any virus-infected plants. Seeds are usually virus-free, so propagate new plants from seed whenever possible.

Botrytis (grey mould)

Using dwarf shrubs with alpines

■ BELOW
Dwarf shrubs, both evergreen and deciduous, form the backbone planting in any rock or scree garden.

Dwarf shrubs are an added bonus in the rock garden, and they provide interest to raised beds and troughs. They are valuable for giving structure, height and form, and they combine extremely well with smaller alpines. Dwarf shrubs come in many different shapes and sizes, ranging from low mounds and buns, to those that are more open and spreading, to cones and pillars, and there are even mat-forming shrubs.

When you are planting a rock garden, it is best to position and plant the shrubs first. They may be regarded as the backbone of the planting scheme, and only when they are satisfactorily positioned can the rest of the space be filled in with alpines and dwarf bulbs. The best time to plant dwarf shrubs is in late autumn or early spring, although evergreen subjects are better left until early spring.

When you are choosing, the most important point to consider is that the shrubs must be slow-growing and truly dwarf. There is nothing worse than dwarf shrubs that quickly outgrow their allotted space and have to be removed after just a few years. Shrubs that grow too large will, in any case, be out of proportion with their surroundings in the alpine garden. Dwarf conifers are a particular case in point, and although many are sold as true dwarfs, in reality they are slow-growing and will eventually become too large for their situation. If you are in doubt, check with an alpine nursery to make sure you get the right ones.

The outstanding shrubs for the alpine garden are the daphnes. The most suitable types form dense little bushes, which are spreading to rounded in shape, and produce an abundance of wonderfully scented blooms in late spring and summer. They are not inexpensive, but they are worth the cost. When you are planning the layout of your rock garden, remember that all daphnes hate being moved once they are established, and they will not respond well to over-pruning.

Alpine shrubs should be treated as any other shrub or tree when it comes to planting. The site should be well prepared and plenty of organic matter added, as well as a sprinkling of bonemeal. The majority of alpine shrubs will be purchased as container-grown plants, so give them a thorough soaking before planting them. Make sure that the shrubs are planted at the same depth as they were in their containers, and keep watering until they establish, especially if the weather turns hot and dry.

Good dwarf shrubs for the rock garden

Abies balsamea 'Nana'
A very slow-growing conifer, which forms a compact, rather spiky, grey-green bun, bearing attractive buds in winter. Height 10–30cm (4–12in), spread 10–50cm (4–20in).

Clematis alpina
(alpine clematis)
One of the few climbers to be allowed on to the rock garden, this is an ideal plant to festoon the larger shrubs or to drape over the rocks. It bears paired, neatly divided leaves. The relatively large, pendent, blue flowers, which appear in spring, have a white centre, and these are followed by attractive fluffy seedheads. Height 2–3m (6–10ft).

Daphne alpina
The upright, deciduous, twiggy shrub with elliptical, greyish leaves bears clusters of fragrant white flowers in the late spring and early summer. Height and spread 40cm (16in).

Daphne arbuscula
This very small, extremely slow-growing, twiggy, evergreen shrub has narrow, rather leathery, shiny, deep green leaves. The clusters of fragrant pink flowers appear in the late spring. This is an excellent trough plant. Height and spread 15cm (6in).

Daphne alpina

Daphne cneorum 'Eximea'

Dryas octopetala

Daphne cneorum 'Eximia'
This daphne forms a low, spreading, evergreen mound, with slender stems densely clothed in narrow, grey-green leaves. Small clusters of deep rose, sweetly fragrant flowers are produced in late spring. Height and spread 20–90cm (8–36in).

Daphne collina
A rather dense, rounded, evergreen shrub with elliptical, rather bristly, grey-green leaves. The flowers, which are pale to mid-pink, are borne in dense clusters in late spring and early summer, occasionally later. Height and spread 60cm (24in).

Daphne tangutica Retusa Group (syn. *D. retusa*)
An evergreen, mound-forming shrub, with deep green, leathery, elliptical leaves. Bears fragrant flowers, in pink and white clusters,

followed by bright, lustrous red berries in spring and summer. Height and spread 50cm (20in).

Dryas octopetala
(mountain avens)
The spreading, mat-forming, evergreen shrub has serrated grey-green leaves that are white beneath. Solitary, white, anemone-like flowers are borne in summer on long stalks, well above the mat, and are followed by fluffy seedheads. Height and spread 7.5–60cm (3–24in).

Erinacea anthyllis
(hedgehog broom)
This extremely spiny plant forms dense hummocks of greyish, spine-tipped stems, bearing small and rather insignificant leaves. The violet-blue pea-flowers are produced in clusters all over the hummock in late spring and early summer. It requires

a sheltered, sun-baked position. Ultimate height and spread 50–40cm (20–16in).

Euryops acraeus
A compact, evergreen shrub with crowded, narrow, silvery grey leaves. The daisy flowers are acid yellow and appear during the summer months. It dislikes windy and exposed positions. Height and spread 40–40cm (16–16in).

Genista sagittalis subsp. *delphinensis*
This prostrate, mat-forming shrub has green stems and rather sparse, elliptical leaves. The bright yellow pea-flowers are borne in clusters from late spring to mid-summer. Height and spread 20–70cm (8–28in).

Genista lydia
This rather graceful shrub, with arching, green, whip-like stems and sparse, small leaves, bears yellow pea-flowers,

Euryops acraeus

Helianthemum

Hypericum olympicum

Salix 'Boydii'

which are crowded on the stems, in late spring and early summer. Height and spread 40–60cm (16–24in).

Helianthemum nummularium (rock rose)
Rock roses are delightful alpine shrubs. They have numerous slender stems, which radiate from a central stock and bear oval, green or grey leaves. In late spring and summer, the flowers, in a wide range of bright colours, resemble miniature cistuses; yellows, pinks, oranges and reds dominate. Many named cultivars are widely available, some larger and more vigorous than others. Height 15–25cm (6–10in), spread 20–50cm (8–20in).

Hypericum olympicum
A sub-shrub with erect, woody-based stems and paired, oval, grey leaves. The large, lemon-yellow flowers

are borne from summer to early autumn. Height and spread 30–40cm (12–16in).

Iberis sempervirens (candytuft)
The shrubby candytuft is a familiar garden plant, forming a rather low, spreading, evergreen shrub with numerous, needle-like, leathery, deep green leaves. The dense, flat clusters of white flowers are borne at the shoot tips from mid- to late spring. Height and spread 30–60cm (12–24in); smaller forms are also available.

Juniperus communis 'Compressa'
The finest conifer for the alpine garden, this makes a dense, pointed, grey-green, pencil-like column. It is excellent for raised beds and troughs. Height 20–75cm (8–30in), spread 5–20cm (2–8in).

Lithodora diffusa (syn. Lithospermum diffusum)
This rather bristly, spreading, evergreen shrub has narrow, deep green leaves. The clusters of salver-shaped flowers, which are borne in late spring and early summer, range from pale to deep blue. It requires an acid to neutral soil. Height and spread 20–50cm (8–25in).

Picea glauca var. albertiana 'Conica'
This widely grown conifer forms a neat, deep green, pyramidal or conical shape, adorned by bright yellow-green new shoots early in the year. Height 50–150cm (20–60in), spread 30–120cm (12–48in). (This is the maximum after many years.)

Rhododendron
There are numerous excellent, small, slow-growing rhododendrons suitable for

the rock garden, the smallest being also good in sinks and troughs. All require a moist, humus-rich, acid soil, and they do not mix particularly well with other alpine shrubs. Try *R. campylogynum* (evergreen), *R. camtschaticum* (deciduous), *R. ferrugineum* (evergreen; alpenrose), *R. hirsutum* (evergreen) or *R. impeditum* (evergreen). There are many others, including lots of named cultivars.

Salix 'Boydii'
A very slow-growing, twiggy, deciduous shrub, with a thick trunk, which eventually looks rather gnarled. The leaves, which are rounded and rather crinkly, are grey-green, and paler beneath. Small, brownish, upright catkins are produced in spring. Height and spread (after many years) 30–60cm (12–24in).

Calendar

Spring

Routine jobs

Protect vulnerable alpines from late frosts; emerging shoots of meconopsis and dwarf rhododendron buds are especially prone to damage. Apply a top-dressing of bonemeal to revitalize the soil. Trim back the early-flowering alpines, such as aubrieta and yellow alyssum, the moment they have finished. Deadhead early-flowering bulbs as they begin to wither, removing any dying or yellowing leaves at the same time; make sure that bulb leaves do not flop on top of choice alpine plants. Remove any dead growth on dwarf shrubs, especially winter die-back; prune into healthy growth, but do not over-prune. At the same time, remove any dead or diseased growth from alpines to prevent the spread of disease; this applies particularly to cushion plants.

Planting and propagation

Start to plant new alpines, making sure that they get ample moisture until they are established. Inspect pots of winter-sown seeds to check for germination, and protect resultant seedlings from the depredations of slugs and snails. Begin to prick out seedlings once they are large enough to handle, and make sure that they are never allowed to dry out. Protect alpines under glass from scorching sun by applying shading; young spring growth is particularly vulnerable.

Summer

Routine jobs

Finish tidying up all spring alpines that have finished flowering, and remove all the remaining dying foliage of spring bulbs. Remember to leave any seedheads, if seed is required. Clip back rock roses after they finish flowering to encourage compact growth with strong shoots for flowering the following year. Keep an eye open for pests and diseases, and take measures to control any that are detected before they become a major problem. Look out for ants, which build nests under alpines and can quickly kill them. Begin collecting seed, labelling each packet carefully; store in a cool, dry place until required. Water the rock garden and troughs regularly during hot, dry weather; a fine mist sprinkler is ideal, and will cause least damage to the plants. Regular weeding will save a lot of time later in the year.

Planting and propagation

Water and feed young pot-grown alpines regularly; the larger ones can

In spring, this *Pulsatilla vulgaris* (pasque flower) bears striking, cup-shaped flowers in shades of red (here, 'Rubra'), pink or white.

be planted out in the garden, and this will give them ample time to become established before winter. Begin to sow seed of those alpines with short viability, such as *Primula*, *Pulsatilla* (pasque flower) and *Ranunculus*, as soon as they are ripe. Take softwood and semi-ripe cuttings of a wide range of alpines during the summer months, as well as rosette cuttings of the cushion types.

Autumn

Routine jobs

Begin to remove fallen leaves from around the rocks and the plants themselves; they can cause alpines to start rotting and may harbour slugs and snails. Deadhead all prolific seeders, such as poppies and *Allium* (onion), to stop them invading the alpine areas too severely. At the same time, collect seed of numerous alpines, making sure it is dry before placing it in labelled envelopes. Clear areas where autumn-flowering bulbs, such as crocuses and cyclamen, are sited. Remove encroaching liverworts and mosses with a proprietary spray, or they will infest the whole area during winter and damage some alpines. Check that cushion alpines in particular have a good collar of rock

chippings under them to help ward off excessive winter moisture.

Planting and propagation

Continue to prick out summer-sown alpines; these will need to be overwintered in a cold frame or glasshouse. Start taking hardwood cuttings, especially of dwarf alpine shrubs, such as *Salix* (willow) and conifers. Protect vulnerable outdoor alpines from winter wet by placing a sheet of glass or Perspex (Plexiglas) over them. Start to sow seed for germinating the following spring. Robust alpines, such as alpine pansies, *Ajuga* (bugle) and primrose cultivars, can be lifted and divided to increase the stock.

Winter

Routine jobs

Complete trimming back old flowering stems and seedheads, growth on herbaceous alpines and fern fronds. Trim back vigorous spreading and mat-forming alpines to make sure that they are not encroaching on less robust neighbours. Take advantage of winter to construct new sites for alpines or to make major renovations to existing ones. Replenish top-dressings of rock chippings around alpines, whether on

the rock garden or in containers, removing weeds and adding a dressing of bonemeal at the same time; be sure to work the chippings in well under each plant whenever possible. Protect vulnerable alpines, such as the early flowering saxifrages, from birds.

Check crevice alpines after severe frosts to make sure that they have not been pushed out of their cracks. Knock any snow off larger alpine conifers if it is likely to break branches or spoil their shape.

Planting and propagation

Clean pots in preparation for spring. Continue to sow alpine seed for spring germination; make sure that both pots and compost (soil mix) are adequately sterilized. Water pots well after sowing and place them in a cold shady part of the garden for germination; a well-aerated cold frame is ideal, but make sure that they are never allowed to dry out.

Index

ACKNOWLEDGEMENTS
The publisher would like to thank
the following for providing images:
Christopher Wilson-Grey: 10, 11,
14b, 15b, 19tl, 19tc, 19tr, 20tl,
20bl, 21tl, 22tl, 24br, 25tl, 25tr,
25bl, 28bl, 31br, 32tr, 33br, 35tl,
36br, 37bl, 46t, 46b, 47tl, 47tr,
53t, 53b, 60l, 60c, 60r, 61l, 63.
The Garden Picture Library: 21bl
(Brian Carter), 22bl (John Glover),
30bl (Neil Holmes), 30br (J S Sira),
31tr (Lynne Brotchie), 32tl
(Sunniva Harte), 33tr (Chris
Burrows), 35tr (John Glover),
36tr (J S Sira), 62 (Chris Burrows).
Harry Smith Collection: 1, 5tr,
19b, 20bc, 22tr, 22br, 23tr, 26t,
26br, 27t, 27bl, 27bc, 27br, 28tr,
29tl, 29bl, 30tr, 31bl, 32bl, 32br,
34tl, 34tr, 34bl, 35bl, 37br.

Sempervivum arachnoideum